How to use Bitcoin to get rich

Building Wealth via Crypto Currencies

Author: Christian A.P. Bartsch

Version: 1.3

Copyright © 2018

ISBN of paperback version:
978-3-947256-02-0

Publisher:

ACATO GmbH
Theresienhoehe 28
80339 Munich
Germany

Copyright © Christian Bartsch 2018

Christian Bartsch has asserted his right to be identified by ACATO GmbH as the author of this work in accordance with the British Copyrights, Designs and Patents Act 1988 and German Copyright laws.

ISBN: 978-3-947256-02-0

Book title: How to use Bitcoin to get rich

First published by ACATO GmbH in 2018:

Version 1 in 2018,

Copyright © 2018 Christian Bartsch, ACATO GmbH

Document published originally: 05 Jan 2018
Document revision for reprint: 21 Jan 2018

Time for Thanksgiving

I would like to thank my Coach **J.T. Foxx** for showing me the way past gauges, mountains and fences that poison your mind-set. When I am stuck with a lot of crazy thoughts, you punch me with your positive mind-set and empower me like a stealth jet.

Thank you **Damien Elston** for teaching as your art of selling and allowing us to buy from you all that knowledge you are providing to us again and again. You are truly a **#212**.

I also thank Coach **Reggie Batts** for getting me more focused and rebuilding my time management. Without time you cannot write a book of value. Without understanding how to get properly coached, you cannot reach the next level. Thank you Reggie.

This is not my first book, but **Coach Francie** taught me some valuable insights on how to offer my knowledge to the world in a book people want to read.

Thanks to **Coach Sean** and **Coach Cherie** I will give my readers the opportunity to experience very unique insights into crypto currencies by inviting them to free one-day events around the world. These great coaches teamed up with **Coach Kevin** and **Coach Brent** to give me advice that helped me change the pace of my crypto currency business.

Needless to say, I also thank Coach Kevin, Coach Brent, Coach **Jeff** K., **Coach Jason** and Coach Joe. Coaches Jason and Brent helped me get prepared to interview Apple Co-founder Steve Wozniak.

Thank you Steve Wozniak for your words of wisdom that will accompany my thoughts when I educate all generations to understand, that innovation does not have to be a threat. Legacy is created by your efforts to make the world a better place.

Thanks also to my business partners and FamilyFirst friends for their support:

John Stokoe, Hajnalka Reon, David Fabricius, Jani & Jenny Pickhan, Nicholas Miaskowski & Family, Christine Nielsen, Ben Chai, Ricardo Hohmann, Marcel Hütten, Shyuan Seah, Gabrielle McKenna & all other FamilyFirst members.

Crypto currencies should be used to help people and not to get rich quickly. Building your digital wealth legacy is more important than the money. You can do a lot more good in this world when you have money.

If **JT Foxx and Damien Elston** had not built a bridge for us all to cross the quicksand dividing the struggling high potentials and the successful people they would have not created this very special group of people who help each other. They are building a legacy for generations to come.

#MineYourWealth

Do what ever it takes to go beyond what imagination can offer as a realistic outcome.

Dedication

I dedicate this book to my Wife, Daughter, and Parents.

Those who have a lot of patience in coaching us – this is also for you.

This is also to my Friends who accompany me along the stony path to success.

Content

1	**INTRODUCTION**	**7**
2	**CRYPTO CURRENCIES EXPLAINED**	**10**
	2.1 CRYPTO CURRENCIES FOR PAYMENTS	12
	2.2 WHICH CRYPTO CURRENCIES EXIST?	13
	2.3 WHY PEOPLE ARE ATTRACTED BY CRYPTO CURRENCIES	14
	2.3.1 Governments want total transparency	14
	2.3.2 Bank data being shared with 100+ countries opens doors to criminals	14
	2.3.3 Freedom by using crypto currencies	17
	2.4 FINANCIAL RISKS OF BITCOIN	18
	2.5 CRYPTO CURRENCY SCAMS	19
	2.5.1 Sample case – OneCoin.eu Scam	20
3	**THE CRYPTO CURRENCY BITCOIN**	**21**
	3.1 USING BITCOIN FOR PAYMENTS	22
	3.2 BUYING BITCOINS	22
	3.3 SELLING BITCOINS	23
	3.3.1 Market places	24
	3.4 HOLDING COINS	24
	3.5 COMPOUNDING BITCOINS	24
4	**TRADING CRYPTO CURRENCIES**	**25**
	4.1 BASIC KNOWLEDGE	25
	4.1.1 Crypto currencies are not part of the regular stock exchange	26
	4.1.2 Beginners might prefer to trade crypto currency stocks at a disadvantage	26
	4.1.3 Easy way to start trading coins	26
	4.1.4 Professionals use powerful trading platforms	26
	4.1.5 The crypto currency markets tend to be high-risk areas of investment	27
	4.1.6 Hedging as a leaver to mitigate portfolio risks	27
	4.1.7 Letting others do the trading for you	27
	4.1.8 Wealth management as an alternative	28
	4.2 GETTING STARTED WITH BASIC TRADING	28
	4.3 GO FROM BASIC TO ADVANCED TRADING SKILLS	29
5	**BITCOIN MINING?**	**30**
	5.1 WHAT IS ACTUALLY MINING?	30

5.2		MINING SPEED	31
5.3		MINING HARDWARE	32
5.4		MINING FARMS	32
5.5		MINING COSTS	33
5.6		MINING ALTERNATIVES	34
	5.6.1	*The CryptoNote family*	34
	5.6.2	*The equihash family*	36
	5.6.3	*The ethash Family*	36
	5.6.4	*The Groestl coin family*	37
	5.6.5	*The Scrypt Family*	37
	5.6.6	*The sha256 Family*	38
	5.6.7	*The X11 Family*	40
	5.6.8	*The X13 family*	42
5.7		MINING TERMS EXPLAINED	43
	5.7.1	*What is a share in the context of pool mining?*	43

6 BITCOIN FOR BUSINESS — 45
- 6.1 USING BITCOIN FOR ECOMMERCE — 45
- 6.2 USING BITCOIN FOR CORPORATIONS — 46
- 6.3 BITCOIN FOR REAL ESTATE INVESTORS — 46
  - 6.3.1 *Blockchain Projects for property investors* — 48

7 WEALTH MANAGEMENT WITH CRYPTO CURRENCIES 48
- 7.1 COMPOUND A PORTFOLIO VIA RULE OF 7 — 49
- 7.2 TRACK OF YOUR CRYPTO CURRENCY PORTFOLIO — 49
- 7.3 UNDERSTAND A PROMISING PORTFOLIO — 50
- 7.4 LEAVE A SINKING SHIP WITH A LIFE VEST — 50
- 7.5 DIVERSIFY AND MITIGATE RISKS — 51
- 7.6 INVEST IN POWERFUL PORTFOLIO EDUCATION — 52

8 GLOBAL TAXATION PERSPECTIVES — 53
- 8.1 TAXATION IN THE AMERICAS — 54
- 8.2 TAXATION IN EUROPE — 55
- 8.3 TAXATION IN ASIA — 57
- 8.4 TAXATION IN THE MIDDLE EAST — 58
- 8.5 TAXATION IN AFRICA — 58

9 ABOUT THE AUTHOR — 58
10 BIBLIOGRAPHY — 60

1 Introduction

Thank you for investing your time to read this book. This is not going to be the typical complex book that only talks about hardware, mathematical formulas, program codes or investment risks.

This is going to open your minds towards the opportunities of using crypto currencies to build step by step a sustainable digital wealth.

If you really want to understand what is happening in the world, you have to move out of your comfort zone. The world of investment is always accompanied by opportunities and risks. This is the case for stock options company shares and crypto currencies.

If you do not understand how crypto currencies can influence your investment then you are exposing yourself to an extremely high risk. You do not need to go to university in order to mitigate your risk.

It is about having the knowledge that you can use to take an idea as an opportunity for investment success. If you think you do not need to take care of your investment portfolio then you are even pushing the developed wealth off the plate as it starts rocking back and forth.

Outside factors can also deface your investment strategy, if it has no flexibility for taking other routes in order to avoid frontal collisions. That is where standard procedures meet flexible approaches.

Legal Information

In accordance with local and national laws of different jurisdictions we are required to highlight the fact that this book is not intended to advise you on legal or tax issues. If you are investing, trading or using crypto currencies for any kind of thing, you may have to ask your tax advisor or a tax expert that specializes on the implications of crypto currencies.

Since crypto currencies are an area that is often very unfamiliar for most financial, tax or legal advisors, you need to understand that you might have to ask a specialized expert to make sure you are not exposing yourself to unnecessary risks.

In general many countries are welcoming the innovation brought about by crypto currency initiatives, nevertheless some countries would like you to declare your profit when you have sold coins.

For more information please refer to the appropriate section of our educational material.

Volatility warnings

When you invest in crypto currencies, mining services or trading services, you are engaging in a high-risk investment area.

You should **never risk money you cannot afford to lose**, since there is a substantial threat that you might incur a financial loss.

2 Crypto currencies explained

When people talk about digital money or crypto currencies they often refer to one of the oldest crypto currencies "Bitcoin". Several programmers and scientists further developed the concept of Blockchain. The first crypto currency system Bitcoin started in January 2009.

Crypto currencies are digital and decentralized payment systems. They make use of the peer-to-peer concept. Payments over a large distance happen faster with crypto currencies than with traditional banking systems.

If you make a payment of 25.000 USD by using the iCamba coin (ICC) it will only cost you about 0.00125 coins. It happens within 30 seconds and this represents a saving of over 1300 USD in comparison to making the same transaction from USA to Europe by using banks.

If you pay approximately 50 EUR using Bitcoin (BTC) it will cost you between 2 USD and 5 USD depending on the current state of the system and the speed you need it done. Sending 14 Pounds from a German EURO Account to the UK cost me in 2015 an astonishing 45 EUR in bank fees. Would I have done it with credit card I would have paid 2 EUR. Doing this today with a currency like "Monero" (XMR) it would have cost me less than 2 EUR.

These examples show that crypto currencies offer a considerable competitive advantage beyond what traditional bank transfers have to offer. Crypto currencies make no difference between the nationality, gender, account rating or other status of a payer. Hence, crypto currencies are way beyond what a democracy has to offer to its citizens today.

A transaction is very easy to do. The seller enters in his smartphone the amount he wants and shows the QR code to his buyer. The buyer can be standing next to him or looking at the QR code while connected through "Teamviewer", "zoom.us" or any video over the Internet service. The buyer activates the payment scanner and scans the displayed QR code. Then he confirms the payment and enters his transaction password. Only then the coins are sent out.

The seller will then see the coins being displayed in his wallet. After a few minutes they will become confirmed and change colour. That is the moment when his balance grows and his wallet allows him to use the received coins for paying others.

By sending the buyer the wallet address as text, a payment can be performed, too. The buyer copies it into his wallet app and enters the amount to be transferred. After confirmation and unlocking the payment is sent.

Due todays low interest rate, people are getting annoyed at banks making huge profits by using their money whilst not giving any interest on their savings. A personal bank account can get into debt and cause considerable bank fees. Since a crypto currency wallet cannot get a negative value it cannot generate debt interest rate fees.

Can a crypto currency wallet not get any interest on compounding values stored inside it? Depending on the crypto currency and the technology used, some wallets are able to generate an interest what adds to the growing wealth of a wallet owner. For this you need special software. Some services require you to keep an amount for 30 to 60 days before rewarding account holders.

This aspect shows how crypto currencies can benefit the general public, retailers, ecommerce businesses and even city councils. Some islands and cities are now accepting crypto currencies as payment, since they see an advantage of getting an easy access to funds that can grow in value.

Even banks and investment funds see it as an opportunity they are carefully testing to understand what they have to do, to regain their competitive advantage.

2.1 Crypto currencies for payments

What makes crypto currencies so competitive in comparison to fiat money? When we refer to fiat money we are actually talking about the analogue currencies such as US Dollars, Euros, Pounds, Zloty, Rupees or other paper money currencies.

The fiat currencies need to be either transferred between a buyer and a seller either by using physical objects (coins or banknotes) or by using bank transfer services (e.g. bank wire, SEPA transfers, Credit cards, etc.). For this old style of transactions only credit cards offer an instant payment to the parties involved. Even a fast bank transfer needs 24 hours to be securely completed.

In the world of crypto currencies you can make a payment instantly and the coins reach directly the sellers wallet. Even though a credit card seems to be instant it is not the case for the seller, as a credit card holder can cancel the transaction after receiving the goods and the credit card service withholds payments for a certain period of time before initiating the bank transfer to the seller.

The seller accepting a crypto currency payment has full control over the coins he was paid within seconds. Hence, he can either keep them there in his wallet or use them to pay someone else. He can also transfer them to a currency conversion server such as "**Changelly**" (got to following address for special offers: www.changelly.com/?ref_id=08876d8826cc).

This conversion service allows you to convert XMR (Monero coins) into BTC (Bitcoins). For the conversion you will be charged small transaction fees. A minimum transaction amount is required. This is currently one of the weaknesses of crypto currencies. As soon as their financial value skyrockets the minimum transaction amount becomes unattractive for small payments (e.g. selling a used cell phone).

2.2 Which crypto currencies exist?

In the world there exist a lot of different crypto currencies. Some are speculative, some are fun and others are looking for their greater purpose.

Release	Name	Code	Algorithm
2009	Bitcoin	BTC	Sha256
2011	Litecoin	LTC	Scrypt
2014	Dash	DASH	X11
2014	Monero	XMR	Cryptonight
2015	Etherium	ETH	Ethash
2016	Zcash	ZEC	Equihash
2017	Bitcoin Cash	BCH	Sha256d
2017	iCambaCoin	ICC	X11

2.3 Why people are attracted by crypto currencies

2.3.1 Governments want total transparency

Since governments are trying to get rid of paper money you have to evaluate what their objective might be. The key issue for the citizens is that if you want to open a political party or want to campaign for protecting the environment, a lobby group can influence the political elite to force the electronic banking systems to freeze your account or deny you the ability to open a bank account.

The ability of governments to remove the banking privacy has already begun as banks are now sending their clients with international transactions a lot of forms to declare why they are receiving these payments.

Even if you decide not to use banks to transfer money abroad, you will see that using other transfer services are also transparent.

If you transfer money by services that allow you to send money to Africa, you will have to fill in a form, in order to declare where you got the money from, what your job is and who you are sending the money and for which purpose.

When you do these transfer systems you are letting people take control of your destiny.

2.3.2 Bank data being shared with 100+ countries opens doors to criminals

In accordance with the OSCE agreements on measures to prevent tax evasion and money laundry, more than 100 countries have agreed to share with each other data of bank account holders. This includes names, account balance, income source and other private data. The bank account holder has no way to stop this intrusion into his privacy.

This leads to the following first 54 countries already sharing the data:

- Anguilla, Argentina, Barbados, **Belgium**, Bermuda, the **British Virgin Islands**, Bulgaria,
- the Cayman Islands, Colombia, Croatia, Curaçao, Cyprus, Czech Republic,
- **Denmark**, Estonia, the Faroe Islands, Finland, **France**,
- **Germany**, Gibraltar, Greece, Greenland, Guernsey,
- Hungary, Iceland, India, Ireland, the Isle of Man, Italy,
- Jersey, Korea, Latvia, **Liechtenstein**, Lithuania, Luxembourg,
- **Malta**, Mexico, Montserrat, **Netherlands**, Niue, Norway, **Poland**, Portugal, Romania,
- San Marino, the Seychelles, the Slovak Republic, Slovenia, **South Africa**, Spain, Sweden,
- Trinidad and Tobago, Turks and Caicos Islands, **United Kingdom**.

In 2018 following 47 countries will gradually join this group:

- Albania, Andorra, Antigua and Barbuda, Aruba, **Australia**, **Austria**, the Bahamas, Bahrain, Belize, Brazil, Brunei Darussalam,
- **Canada**, Chile, China, Cook Islands, Costa Rica, Dominica,
- Ghana, Grenada, Hong Kong (China), Indonesia, Israel, **Japan**, Kuwait, Lebanon,
- the Marshall Islands, Macao (China), Malaysia, Mauritius, Monaco, Nauru, New Zealand, Panama, Qatar, Russia,

15

- Saint Kitts and Nevis, Samoa, Saint Lucia, Saint Vincent and the Grenadines, Saudi Arabia, Singapore, Sint Maarten, **Switzerland**,

- **Turkey**, the **United Arab Emirates**, Uruguay and Vanuatu.

This agreement by government officials has a significant impact on wealthy and exposed people. This can endanger the lives of dissidents, political adversaries, entrepreneurs, innovators, political refugees, veterans and even people you would not expect to be at risk.

From a privacy perspective you need to see this as a considerable intrusion into peoples lives and company secrets. Since the list of countries also includes countries suffering from massive corruption and crime, you have to accept that your governments might not have thought of the risks they are exposing their people to. When criminals want access to this kind of data they **will bribe officials** in order to get **extensive profiles** of interesting people they can try to target.

With this information they can go to pinpoint their criminal projects to the extent that they are able to maximize their financial profits, as they are <u>well aware about their victim's financial balance</u>. Whether they desire to use extortion, blackmail, theft, mule based fraud schemes or even hijacking … their information is up to date.

This also allows criminals in the Ransomware field to direct their spear fishing efforts towards targets that are worthwhile and offer potential weaknesses. In 2015-2016, criminals in different countries collected over 13 million USD in ransom used Ransomware attacks. Instead of getting paid by bank transfers or cross-country payment services, they tried to escape detection by hording crypto currencies.

Their **victims had to buy Bitcoins** in order to pay the criminals with the hope to get their data decrypted. At that time 1 Bitcoin was valued between 400 USD and 700 USD. The collected ransom is mostly hidden, waiting to be cashed. Some experts see this as a **volatility risk for the Bitcoin** as the ransom has not been converted into any other currency by most of the criminals.

Unfortunately, you will not be able to change the decisions of the authorities, as they believe they are building a defence system against money laundering. The only real thing an individual and any company can do is to venture into the world of crypto currencies to gain some time by making use of more confidential systems.

Further more you must be aware that there exist systems you can use to **track an individual's crypto currency activities**. Many crypto currencies are either not sufficiently encrypted or partly encrypted. This is also a weakness of the Bitcoin which shoes that some people believe the Bitcoin is so encrypted that no outsider is able to look into their payment activities.

2.3.3 Freedom by using crypto currencies

If you do not want that banks, insurance companies or politicians have control over your life you will need to look for an alternative to cash. Governments will remove cash from our lives.

Hence, you need to get into crypto currencies. Successful people are moving their wealth from banks and placing it in different wallets inside the crypto currency world.

Even people who are not actively interested in computer stuff are now rushing into the digital world with their money.

These are multi millionaires who know how important it is to keep your wealth to yourself. Out there are people who do not like if you own a Porsche or a cool bike. When they see an opportunity they will try to throw negativity at you. Some people do this by scratching your car. Others post bad things in the Internet about you.

But do you want others to decide whether you will be successful and happy in life? No, so do not let yourself be driven into their negative mind-set.

When you use crypto currencies for making payments you regain your privacy to a certain extent. Nevertheless, not every currency is fully encrypted. Bitcoin transactions can be traced using specialized forensic software. Get educated on the pros and cons of the currencies you want to invest and use for payments.

2.4 Financial risks of Bitcoin

In the world of crypto currencies there is not only the risk of falling for a scam, but also the risk of loosing money by suffering due to devaluation of a particular crypto currency.

As an example let us look at the most pushed currency Bitcoin:

In 2015 the Bitcoin ranged between 300 USD and 800 USD. It quickly lifted up to an area between 1.400 and 2.500 USD. In 2017 we experienced the hype that drove the Bitcoin price up to 3.000, then 5.000 and then 10.000 USD. In December 2017 it even jumped within weeks from 11.000 to 20.000 USD.

So what is the risk accompanied by such sudden valuation hypes? Everything that goes in extreme directions will keep changing its directions with sudden massive bursts.

So financially speaking the Bitcoin has become a speculative currency that poses extreme volatility risks. Yes, you can gain a lot of money whilst exposing yourself to potential risks.

If you tend to jump into a currency opportunity by buying coins then your unexpected loss may be considerably high if you buy the currency at the wrong moment. If you are experienced in speculating with stock options and company shares, then you should know that you have to look for the indicators that show you when a drop is to be expected.

You need to buy when it is low and sell when it is high at its peak but not yet going to fall. This way you can take advantage of the waves occurring on the market.

If you prefer to build you wealth using a diversification strategy then that is where you have to look towards crypto currency hedging. The strategies and methods for doing so are highly specialized but can be learned by any person willing to invest in the necessary crypto currency mastermind and trainings.

2.5 Crypto currency scams

When you become interested to invest in crypto currencies, you will become bombarded by lots of different offers to invest in Bitcoins. When you are looking towards diversifying your investments you might look into new coin offerings (so called ICO's).

Unfortunately there is a lot of fraud going on in the digital world.

Here is a brief selection of scams that have been highlighted recently (CoinScamList, 2017):

- A3M Alexander iii magnus (Open Markets)
- BCO Bridgecoin (Open Markets)
- BRA Brazil (Open Markets)
- BSDB Bsdbmoney (Open Markets)
- CAN Caninet (Open Markets)
- COLX Colossuscoinxt (Open Markets)
- DFS Dfscoin (Open Markets)
- DMX Darkmatter (Open Markets)
- EDGAR Edgarcoin (Open Markets)
- EPR Eprcoin (Open Markets)
- ETHD Etheriumdark (Open Markets)
- GNB Giantbird (Open Markets)
- GOKU Gokucoin (Open Markets)
- NELSON Nelsonmandela
- POS Pos (Open Markets)
- PWC Playwincoin (Open Markets)
- SiM Simcoin (Open Markets)
- SK21 SkullEvollution (Open Markets)
- TZC Trezarcoin (Open Markets)
- VEGA Vegacoin (Open Markets)
- VOLKS Volkswagen
- VSX Vsync (Open Markets)

2.5.1 Sample case – OneCoin.eu Scam

The "OneCoin.eu" was a crypto currency scam **based on an MLM** (Multi Level Marketing) platform (Suberg, 2016). The interesting thing about this particular scam is that people tend to refer to this scam when they see new coins they are suspicions off.

This scam was **faking its coins and wallets** all the time. There was never a system that allowed you to move coins between wallets and there was <u>no real crypto currency system in place</u>.

The criminals behind this scam were actually based in Bulgaria. Their directors were already known for having been running other scams in the past. Their previous involvement with the "Crypto888" and the "Brilliant Carbon" scam tainted the management team of Onecoin. Therefore it became apparent that their scam was using a pyramid scheme to build the structure necessary to make enormous gains.

According to a Wikipedia record the authorities were able to recover $3.66 million USD but the majority of the gathered gains (approx. $11.16 million USD) were never recovered (Wikipedia, 2017).

3 The Crypto Currency Bitcoin

When people talk about digital money or crypto currencies they often refer to one of the oldest crypto currencies "Bitcoin".

Satoshi Nakamoto started the first crypto currency system in January 2009. At that time it was more of a nerds' play money, as many years the general public did not take the concept seriously. Today people are going mad about Bitcoin as it was during the gold rush. People gamble all their savings for a get rich quickly attitude.

As a decentralized crypto currency the Bitcoin makes use of the peer-to-peer concept. Hereby it removes government control over payment transactions. Bitcoin is faster that old style bank transfers.

Bitcoin is often referred to as a foreign currency. Government cannot print a Bitcoin. No financial institute governs the quantity of coins released into the market.

You can compare a Bitcoin wallet to a PayPal account or a Credit card account. You can only spend as much as you are allowed. If you don't have Bitcoins in your wallet you cannot get in debt by overspending. Hence, a crypto currency wallet acts like a debit card or a prepaid credit card.

The amount of Bitcoins is limited to 21 million Bitcoins. This creates scarcity and influences the valuation.

3.1 Using Bitcoin for payments

In order to make payments with Bitcoins you need to have a crypto currency wallet that is compatible with the currency you are intending to use to pay somebody. You need to have the amount of Bitcoins you are intending to send somebody. You also have to have a little more in order to cover the transaction fees.

3.2 Buying Bitcoins

In order to buy Bitcoins you can use a variety of services:

- Exchange platforms
- Conversion services (e.g. payeer.com)
- Bitcoin ATMs (e.g. Cardiff (UK), Linz (AT), ...)
- Trading platforms
- Bitcoin holders
- Bitcoin miners
- Etc.

When you purchase Bitcoins then the coins will be added to your wallets one single time. You will not get more coins if you leave them without other activity.

What is the best platform to buy coins from?

Exchange platforms are fast but charge fees. The price of the Bitcoin is regulated by the current market price.

When you buy Bitcoins from a person, then you need to agree upon a price. This price may be higher or lower than on an exchange platform. Nevertheless, the core advantage is that you will not pay a conversion fee to the seller.

If you want to get a certain value of coins then buying them from a mining company offers you an advantage because their production cost might be lower than the market price of the particular coin.

If you want to increase your balance you either have to buy more coins or invest in a mining pool. I am often asked what is the best strategy to build your wealth by using crypto currencies. You need to use a diversified strategy in order to grow your portfolio while leveraging the risks of such potentially volatile investment opportunities.

3.3 Selling Bitcoins

When you have a wallet with crypto currencies you can use a variety of exchange services to quickly convert coins into other currencies. One of those fast services is "bitstamp". This service is able to convert your coins in real time. This could be called a basic version of trading.

Once you have converted your coins into a fiat currency (e.g. USD or EUR) then you can use the transfer service to send the funds to your bank account. You could even use those funds to purchase other types of coins.

3.3.1 Market places

Localbitcoins.com

Here you can sell and buy coins from other individuals. In order to purchase such coins you can pay in cash or by making a bank transfer.

Kraken.com

This American crypto currency exchange is also quite popular. Verification of your identity can take up to 2-4 days.

3.4 Holding coins

You can keep coins you have bought in a wallet as long as you desire. The stored coins will not decrease as crypto currency wallets do not charge account fees like you would usually have to pay to a bank for having a bank account.

3.5 Compounding Bitcoins

When you mine crypto currencies you can leave the coins in the wallet. Hereby you gradually compound your coins and eventually start selling 25% of old stock each month to generate a passive income. Nevertheless, you need to keep your coin balance under control.

By using special software for compounding, you can increase the amount of coins over a certain time. You will then see how your compounded money is used to generate a sort of interest rate between 0.5% and 5.0% depending on your handling of this crypto currency wallet.

4 Trading Crypto Currencies

Some people buy coins and leave them in their wallets for years. Alternatively, people use mining to grow the amount of coins in their wallets.

Others make use of the market imbalances. They buy coins where they are offered cheaply and then sell them at the exchange with the highest selling price.

In December 2017 the Bitcoin as valued in 2 exchanges with a price difference of 800 USD. If you have sufficient capital to buy enough Bitcoins you can earn within seconds thousands of dollars. The trading systems provide similar diagrams like that of trading systems used for stock options and shares.

4.1 Basic knowledge

This section will provide you with the necessary awareness for a responsible usage of trading services.

4.1.1 Crypto currencies are not part of the regular stock exchange

The Chicago stock exchange started trading Bitcoins inside the frame of a futures contract. This CBOE "futures contract" does not actually involve Bitcoin. There are securities that will track the price of Bitcoin on the largest Bitcoin exchange Gemini.

4.1.2 Beginners might prefer to trade crypto currency stocks at a disadvantage

The tendency to trade stocks instead of currencies is due to people's previous experience of owning a few shares of traditional companies. Here beginners can buy shares from GBTC, which is a trust that owns Bitcoins and sells shares of it. This is a way to avoid having to trade crypto currencies.

The GBTC is being **traded at a premium** so that it would be cheaper to buy coins rather than buying GBTC shares. Furthermore, it is possible to trade crypto currencies in a 24-hour market. This is not possible with traditional stock market where shares cannot be sold at any time of the week.

4.1.3 Easy way to start trading coins

Using services like Coinbase makes it easier for beginners to start trading their crypto currencies. The key disadvantage is that you cannot exchange all crypto currencies and therefore are limited to a handful of mainstream currencies.

4.1.4 Professionals use powerful trading platforms

If you want to increase your profits then you will have to upscale your trading options. This is why professionals go to services like Kraken, Binance, Bittrex, or GDAX.

4.1.5 The crypto currency markets tend to be high-risk areas of investment

If you are intending to use crypto currency trading to increase your wealth, then you need to be aware, that some currencies are extremely volatile in their trading prices. This is particularly the situation with Bitcoin, which is not only traded by investors but also being hoarded by criminals waiting to sell off their ransom money.

4.1.6 Hedging as a leaver to mitigate portfolio risks

With a desire to make a fortune by investing and trading crypto currencies, you need to apply a highly diversified strategy. Hereby, you spread your risks across a variety of mainstream and niche crypto currencies. The way you structure your portfolio depends very much how much leverage power you are creating in your mitigation currencies in order to deflect negative impacts from investing in extreme risk currencies such as Bitcoin.

4.1.7 Letting others do the trading for you

There are several market leaders in the field of automated trading of crypto currencies. If you are contacted by some of their fans, you will notice that their business is being boosted by the power of multi level marketing. This leads to a part of your investment not reaching its target, as the MLM system might offer a complex commission payment plan. If you are happy in joining such a system then you can earn considerable funds by letting them trade for you and by getting others to join the platform, which will generate commissions for you.

4.1.8 Wealth management as an alternative

You can do the trading yourself or buy future contracts or place your bets on automatic trading services. If you just want to let your investment work for you as a passive income then you might also consider letting professionals increase your crypto currency wealth as known by the services of funds and wealth management services.

The downside of such investment funds is the high management fees that are charged by the fund managers. You tend to get little insight into their investment strategies.

That is why it is so important to look into an alternative form of wealth management. Investing into crypto currencies becomes so easy that wealth continues to build up without you having to know all the current trends and technologies in depth. A **VIP wealth management** can offer investors an educational insight into current strategies that can also be applied outside the world of crypto currencies.

4.2 Getting started with basic trading

When you want to start trading crypto currencies, then you should focus on a major currency such as Bitcoin.

Get a user account at **www.coinbase.com** and start buying moderately. Do a few selling transactions to get familiar with the systems peculiarities. This ensures that when you upscale your trading volume you do not loose all your money due to being inexperienced.

Once you have provided the personal identification documents then your trading limits will be lifted. Keep in mind that trading also results in trading fees. Based on the volume you are trading the lower the fees will impact your overall profit margin.

Protect your account by using a **2-factor authentication** so that hackers and data thieves cannot rob you of your wealth whilst you sleep.

By charging up your coinbase account with a budget, you can speed up the trading process. If you use your bank account to fund every trade, you will loose time and money. Bank transfers take 2 – 4 days on average. Besides, having a budget ensures that you do not exceed this budget.

Also make use of the alerts the system provides. By using their app you can do your trading from your phone from any place in the world.

4.3 Go from basic to advanced trading skills

Once you have got familiar with coinbase trading, you should consider moving on to the more flexible platform GDAX, which is also operated by coinbase. This is a healthy way to work on your trading experience whilst keeping away from high risks as long as you are not a trading expert.

Careless trading can lead to burning an entire portfolio within an hour. Such silliness has driven people into insanity. Repeating this stupidity is insane. So keep away from "get rich quickly" formulas that only favour the bank.

For those who feel ready for the masterpiece, it will be time to move onto Binance and Bittrex. These platforms require considerable knowledge and skills to build wealth and not destroy it. This is where **masterminds** and specialized education will help to crack the **magic formula of trading**.

5 Bitcoin Mining?

So that a crypto currency system can supply its users with coins, it needs help from outside. Hereby data centres provide the computation capacity needed to generate the unique hash values that help ensure a coin is not fake coin.

5.1 What is actually mining?

Computers get mathematical puzzles in order to calculate a given hash value. In order to do so, they need to follow given standard procedures. These operating rules tell the mining software which mathematical calculations to work through.

Bitcoin uses the old sha256 algorithm. If your hardware is to mine a valid Bitcoin you need to work through the computation rules of this algorithm. If your system makes a mistake then you will not be rewarded with the mining output.

Once your calculations are complete, the software delivers its results and the crypto currency will process the output. After this the algorithm process confirmation kicks in. Other systems will also confirm that all procedures of calculation are correct. Only then your output will move to your crypto currency wallet. Once the minimum required amount of confirmations have been received, then your wallet balance will grow.

5.2 Mining speed

Often you will see mining services using speed values in different ways:

- 1 H/s is 1 hash per second.
- 1 kH/s is 1,000 hashes per second.
- 1 MH/s is 1,000,000 hashes per second.
- 1 GH/s is 1,000,000,000 hashes per second.
- 1 TH/s is 1,000,000,000,000 hashes per second.
- 1 PH/s is 1,000,000,000,000,000 hashes per second.

Some mining companies take the complexity of hash rates away as they are often misleading. When the difficulty level increases, a 1 GH/s may be no longer profitable. Hence, if you are stuck with one fixed speed you have no change to speed up other than buying a larger package.

Depending on their service offerings and terms they often will upgrade their equipment in order to stay competitive. This is where clients might gain a speed increase or a price reduction.

5.3 Mining hardware

In order to mine your own crypto currencies you can use all sorts of hardware. Depending on the difficulty level of the desired currency you may be able to mine a coin with a computer or a smartphone. If it is very complicated you have to use Graphic cards (GPU) or an ASIC computer.

In todays world of Bitcoin mining you need to use ASIC miners. Yes, you can buy one in the Internet and run it at home. If you have no negotiation power then you will pay a high electricity bill for such little output that it is not worth buying the hardware. It is crazy when you see people offering hardware at double the price, which the hardware actually costs from the manufacturer.

The key weakness of ASIC hardware for Bitcoin mining is that you cannot configure to use it to mine other currencies using more modern algorithms such as X11.

5.4 Mining farms

When you hear people speaking about mining farms then it is the equivalent term to the term "data centres". A farm is a group of mining computers inside a physical location.

A farm may have all sorts of hardware such as ASIC miners, GPU and CPU miners. Even MPU miners might be located there. Some mines have a 100 and others have more than 100.000 devices working day and night to generate coins of different currencies.

5.5 Mining costs

Just plugging in a crypto currency mining device into the next power socket is not sufficient to ensure that a device will last long and deliver an acceptable output.

Hence, like in any type of data centre you have to maintain the hardware and the surrounding infrastructure. Having customized racks, special fire extinguishing systems and the skilled workers, results in operational costs. Devices will get damaged and need to be fixed or replaced.

This results in the following types of operational costs:

- Power costs
- Management costs
- Maintenance costs
- Infrastructure costs
- Fire protection costs

It is not enough to have a building and a few devices. You need to cool the devices and also see how you can reduce the risks to any 3rd party. Continuity plans and mobile emergency data centres are often part of any large enterprise that knows its dependence on its servers and data.

Every data centre needs to be managed so that the operations do not experience a loss of up time or data. Ensuring that your employees are trained and that the systems are set up in a responsible way requires clear instructions.

It is not possible to expect that routine will improve security. Regular scenario trainings and fire exercises should be part of the safety precautions.

This important part of the business creates costs but protects the business from a total loss of its key assets.

5.6 Mining alternatives

Before we can look into mining other types of crypto currencies, we need to understand that there are different types of crypto currency families.

Release	Name	Code	Algorithm
2009	Bitcoin	BTC	Sha256
2011	Litecoin	LTC	Scrypt
2014	Dash	DASH	X11
2014	Monero	XMR	Cryptonight
2015	Etherium	ETH	Ethash
2016	Zcash	ZEC	Equihash
2017	Bitcoin Cash	BCH	Sha256d
2017	iCambaCoin	ICC	X11

5.6.1 The CryptoNote family

The CryptoNote currency family uses the CryptoNight algorithm.

Release	Name	Code	Remarks
	AEON	AEON	Minable. Aimed at delivering fast and secure payments. While being easy to use
2012 July	**Bytecoin**	BCN	Minable. First implementation of CryptoNote technology
	Boolberry	BBR	This is an experiment
	DarkNetCoin	DNC	Platform for anonymous applications such as p2p, gabling, and bets.
2014 July	Dashcoin	DSH	Minable. Key difference is supply amount
	DigitalNote	XDN	Formerly known as DarkNote / Ducknote. Untraceable encrypted messaging system
	DoctorByte	DB	Coin is dead.
	Dosh	DOSH	Untraceable payments; Block analysis resistance
	Fantomcoin	FCN	Minable.

35

			Has merged mining support
	Infinium-8	INF8	Minable. Privacy centric coin
	Magnatoj	XMN	Formerly known as "OneEvilCoin". Untraceable payments use ring signatures
2014	**Monero**	XMR	Minable. Formerly known as Bitmonero. Values: on privacy, decentralization and fungibility. Focuses on decentralization and scalability.
	MonetaVerde	MCN	Block reward increases with difficulty
	Pebblecoin	XPB	Implements mining algorithm "Boulderhash", that requires 13GB RAM. This protects if against botnet controlled computers for mining. Standard block reward is 300 coins.
	Quazarcoin	QCN	Flatter emission curve. Focus on usability of the currency.
	RedWind	RD	

Release	Name	Code	Comments
	Tavos	XTV	

5.6.2 The equihash family

Release	Name	Code	Comments
	BitcoinZ		Not Minable
	Bitcoin Gold	BCG	Minable
	Bitgem		Minable
	Hush		Minable
	Komodo		Minable
	Zcash	ZEC	Minable
	Zclassic		Minable
	Zero		Minable

5.6.3 The ethash Family

Release	Name	Code	Comments
	Bowhead		Not Minable
	DaxxCoin		Minable
	Elementrem		Minable
	Ellaism		Not Minable
	Ethereum		Minable
	Ethereum classic		Minable
	Expanse		Minable
	Musicoin		Minable
	WhaleCoin		Not Minable

5.6.4 The Groestl coin family

Release	Name	Code	Comments
	Groestl coin		Minable

5.6.5 The Scrypt Family

Release	Name	Code	Comments
	Coin		Minable
	BitCoin Plus		Minable
	Bitcoin scrypt		Minable
	Bitconnect		Minable
	DigiByte		Minable
	DogeCoin		Minable
	Fastcoin		Minable
	GoldCoin		Minable
	KiloCoin		Minable
	LiteCoin	LTC	Minable
	Megacoin		Minable
	Noblecoin		Minable
	Russiacoin		Minable
	Shadowcoin		Minable
	Verge		Minable

5.6.6 The sha256 Family

Release	Name	Code	Comments
	808Coin		Minable
	Acoin		Minable
	AnarchistsPrime		Minable
	AntiBitcoin		Minable
	ATBCoin		Not Minable
	Auroracoin		Minable
	Betacoin		Minable
	BitBean		Minable
	Bitcoin		Minable
	Bitcoin Cash		Minable
	BitcoinDask		Minable
	BitSerial		Not Minable

Bittokens	Minable
Breakout	Minable
C-bit	Minable
Californium	Minable
CaliphCoin	Minable
Clinton	Minable
Crown	Minable
Cubits	Minable
DAO.Casino	Minable
Deutsche eMark	Minable
DevCoin	Minable
DigiByte	Minable
Dollarcoin	Minable
EDR Coin	Minable
Emercoin	Minable
EuroCoin	Minable
Fonzecoin	Minable
FireFlyCoin	Minable
Flavorcoin	Minable
Freicoin	Minable
GrantCoin	Minable
High Voltage	Minable
HunterCoin	Minable
IncaKoin	Minable
Infinity Economics	Not Minable
Internet of People	Minable
IOcoin	Minable
Ixcoin	Minable
Joulecoin	Minable
LeaCoin	Minable
LePen	Not Minable
Mazacoin	Minable
Mind Gene	Minable
NameCoin	Minable
Neoscoin	Not Minable

	Neutron		Not Minable
	Pascal Lite		Minable
	ParkByte		Minable
	PayCoin		Not Minable
	ProCurrency		Minable
	Prysmchain		Minable
	PRYZM		Not Minable
	PX		Minable
	Revenu		Minable
	Save and gain		Minable
	Sharkcoin		Minable
	SixEleven		Minable
	Sling		Minable
	Sprouts		Minable
	Swing		Minable
	TEKcoin		Minable
	TerraCoin		Minable
	Tigercoin		Minable
	Titcoin		Minable
	Theresa May Coin		Not Minable
	Unbreakable Coin		Minable
	Universal Currency		Minable
	Unobtanium		Minable
	Ultimate Secure Cash		Not Minable
	X-coin		Minable
	XAUcoin		Minable
	Zayedcoin		Minable
	ZetaCoin		Minable

5.6.7 The X11 Family

Release	Name	Code	Comments
	AdzCoin		Minable
	AmberCoin		Minable

	Coin		Status
	Artex Coin		Minable
	B3Coin		Not Minable
	BeatCoin		Minable
	BitSend		Minable
	BlackStar		Not Minable
	BlueCoin		Minable
	BnrtxCoin		Minable
	Bolivarcoin		Minable
	Boolberry	BBR	Not minable
	BowsCoin		Minable
	Braincoin		Minable
	Capricoin		Minable
	Chaincoin	CHC	
	Colossuscoin V2		Not Minable
	Cream		Minable
	CrevaCoin		Not Minable
	CryptCoin		Minable
	Cycling Coin		Minable
	DAS		Minable
	DarkLisk		Minable
2014	**Dash**	DASH	Minable
	DigitalPrice		Minable
	E-Dinar Coin		Not Minable
	Enigma		Minable
	Eryllium		Minable
	EuropeCoin		Minable
	Evilcoin		Minable
	ExclusiveCoin	EXCL	
	FuelCoin		Not Minable
	GAIA		Not Minable
	GanjaCoin		Minable
	Gay coin		Minable
	GoldBlocks		Minable
	GoldReserve		Minable
	GraniteCoin	GRN	

	Halloween coin		Minable
	HappyCoin		Minable
	Hitcoin		Minable
	Hyperstake		Minable
	Kurrent		Minable
	KushCoin		Minable
2017	**iCambaCoin**	ICC	Minable. This coin focuses on retail and desired to help broke people get out of debt.
	Impact		Minable
	inflationcoin		Minable
	Influxcoin		Minable
	insaneCoin		Minable
	IslaCoin		Minable
	MarxCoin		Minable
	MarsCoin		
	Memetic	MEME	
	Monacocoin		Not Minable
	MonateryUnit	MUE	Minable
	Onix		Minable
	Octanox		Minable
	PeaceCoin		Not Minable
	Pepecoin		
	PiggyCoin		Minable
	Pinkcoin	PINK	Minable
	PizzaCoin		Minable
	Pura		
	QuebeCoin		Not Minable (Quebec)
	RateCoin		Minable
	RegalCoin		Not minable
	Renos		Not Minable

Name	Code	Comments
SportsCoin		Not Minable
Startcoin	START	Minable
SuperCoin		Minable
Sync		Minable
Syndicate		Minable
Synergy		Minable
Tellurion		Minable
TorCoin		Minable
TransferCoin		Minable
TrustCoin		
TruckCoin		Minable
VaultCoin		Minable
Virtacoinplus		Minable
WayGuide		Not Minable
WMCoin		Not Minable
XenixCoin		Minable
ZSECoin		Minable

5.6.8 The X13 family

Release	Name	Code	Comments
	Blitzcash		Not Minable
	Britcoin		Minable
	CloakCoin		Not Minable
	DeepOnion		Minable
	KoreCoin		Not Minable
	MarteXcoin		Minable
	NavCoin		Not Minable
	Stealthcoin		Minable
	Stratis		Not Minable
	Triangles		Minable

5.7 Mining terms explained

5.7.1 What is a share in the context of pool mining?

In crypto currency mining there are mining pools in the crypto currency system and as mining communities. Here you might read or hear about a mining share that is not acting as you thought to have understood what shares are. This is due to the fact, that when people talking about crypto currencies and mining shares they are mixing up different kind of terms and therefore using one term to describe different objects.

In the technical context of mining (pools):

A share is a block "solution" **not sufficient to be published** as an actual block. This is still a valuable contribution to the community as it's really hard to find blocks. This means that shares can be used to measure how much work the mining hardware is doing. This is a measure with **much finer and more consistent granularity** than actual block solutions, which are far too rare for small miners.

Here an example for a better understanding:

Suppose that the current difficulty was 10,000. To become valid blocks, an attempted block with a specific nonce has to be "better" than 10,000.

In this situation, the pool might set their "share difficulty" at 100. So with each nonce the mining system attempts, the mining software will check to see how "good" the difficulty of the resulting block is. Most of these blocks will be below 100 in "difficulty level", but a small amount of them will be over 100 in difficulty level (and still less than 10,000).

These special blocks are called "shares". They can be sent into the mining pool, even though they aren't good enough to be published on the open network as actual blocks. Inside these shares the mining pool will be clearly marked as the recipient of any potential block reward, which means that the mining pool can use the number of shares you submit as clear evidence of how much work your machine is doing to try and find blocks for the pool, **EVEN IF YOU'VE NEVER FOUND ONE YET**. Which is good, because it takes forever to find actual blocks.

As the mining continues submitting shares, eventually a solution will be found that is not only good enough to be a share, it's actually good enough to be a real block! That is, it has difficulty "over 10,000" and so it meets not just the share criteria but also the full network standard of difficulty, which is much harder.

This one you would still submit to the pool, but when they get it they will go ahead and publish it out over the actual network, receiving a **substantial reward** that gets distributed amongst everyone according to the shares they've been submitting. Most software works by just telling the mining machine to look for blocks over 100 and not worry about what the network difficulty is. But still, we can see how someone who isn't doing actual mining would never be able to find any shares in the first place, which means this is actually reasonably secure from the pool's perspective as a way of measuring how much work everyone is doing.

Above example does not acknowledge a lot of details of mining, because there are some subtle tricks the pool needs to be careful of.

In a nutshell this is what shares actually are: totally normal blocks that **don't meet the full requirements** to be published on the network, but still meet some smaller requirement set by the pool to count as proof you're mining with the pool set as the recipient.

Now, why can't the miner just submit any actual blocks themselves to take the whole reward?

Two reasons: first, in order for their shares to be valid they have to have the pool set as the recipient, so the mined block already gives the reward to the pool no matter who broadcasts it, and second the pool doesn't actually bother giving the whole block out to miners. It is just a template for the header that contains the hashes of the actual block contents.

6 Bitcoin for Business

6.1 Using Bitcoin for eCommerce

Can you use Bitcoin for ecommerce? Yes, several companies have been offering solutions for online shops so that they can diversify their payment offers beyond what credit cards and PayPal have to offer. Nevertheless, the number of offline retailers willing to risk their revenues by accepting Bitcoin is very low.

One of the key weaknesses of Bitcoin is that transactions are becoming very slow and costly. Due to the high selling price of Bitcoin a small transaction of 50 USD might result in a 5 USD transaction fee. When retailers are selling low priced goods this fee destroys the advantage of using crypto currencies. Therefor selling coffee for 2 USD and paying 5 USD transaction fees is economically insane. Other coins are offering faster and cheaper transactions by applying more efficient algorithms such as the X11.

6.2 Using Bitcoin for Corporations

Why are some corporations looking into using Bitcoins for intercompany transactions across the world? If a company transfers 25.000 USD from the USA to France it will cost approximately 1.500 USD in bank fees. You also loose pat of the transaction value due to conversion of USD to EUR as the recipient has a EURO based bank account.

Hence, using Bitcoin or any other trustable crypto currency can offer considerable annual cost reduction as the banking fees of several millions are reduced by "1/10000", which is a competitive advantage for early adopters. Nevertheless, corporations need some time to become familiar with crypto currencies.

6.3 Bitcoin for Real Estate Investors

Having discussed the opportunities presented by Bitcoin and its Blockchain technology, entrepreneurs are searching for new ways to apply Blockchain technology in their individual industries. The idea of manifesting purchase and lease contracts by using block chain technology does not really require the use of Bitcoin. This is due to its high fluctuation and slow processing.

Besides in some countries the data privacy weaknesses of Bitcoin may be a cause for investors to hold back. One key advantage for a globally focused real estate investor is that he does not need to make costly bank transfers from his home country to a foreign location where he intends to buy or lease property.

Hence, the purchase of a property might be occurring via a BTC payment or a BTC to local currency conversion transaction. When we refer to a BTC payment, a transfer of Bitcoins from the buyer's wallet to the seller's wallet is being processed. The seller gets the Bitcoins into his wallet within a short time and knows that the buyer cannot take the coins away again.

When a conversion transaction is happening, it becomes a much more complex process than often desired by the buyer. Hereby, the buyer has to transfer the Bitcoins to a conversion platform. There he can either directly convert it or has to find other people willing to exchange it for local currency. Hereby he may loose part of the value of his funds. After converting he then has to transfer the local currency to a local bank account. In some countries this can lead to loss of time and increased transfer costs.

Nevertheless, a real estate investor can take advantage of crypto currencies by applying the appropriate strategies that make him a quick mover. Thereby he can buy a property at a lower price before any competitor can make an offer. This easiness of property transaction empowers the investor to the extent that he can increase his profits way beyond industry standards. When a global investor is dealing with unfamiliar jurisdictions he or she has to make sure they are not running into legal traps as they might loose their right to the property.

In any global business venture you need to make sure when buying a property abroad that you are dealing with the owner and not an impersonator. Once you have sent your Bitcoins to the other party you are not able to reverse the transaction if you find out that it was a scam.

Do not get burned by criminals using identity theft to pretend to be the owner of the property. If you are interested in the strategies of real estate investors then participating in one of the below listed training and masterminds will give you the knowledge you need to apply niche tools to your advantage.

6.3.1 Blockchain Projects for property investors

With the help of leading international property investors we are now adapting this technology. The new concept will increase the financial power of the investor so that he can start small projects around the world and quickly use these projects to finance larger projects. This will open opportunities to <u>buy, flip and refinance real estate</u> properties at a greater scale.

Hereby tools from the banking and corporate world are being used to generate powerful financial instruments (Asset backed securities, compounding, rule of 7) that can be used anywhere in the world. With the expertise of leading authorities in the field of **property investment** a digital shortcut to wealth creation is being designed. This is where passive income from property investments can speed up the time needed for reaching several levels of net worth.

7 Crypto Wealth Management

When you intend to build your wealth then you should apply a series of strategies. You can outsource your wealth management or attempt to build such a system by yourself.

7.1 Compound a portfolio via Rule of 7

One of the most powerful ways is by applying the rule of 7. This particular rule is often seen in connection with credit card debts, which are charged at 22% in some countries. Hereby, banks can bind the client to a long debt agreement that will compound over a long period. This leads to debt doubling on average every 7 years. The slower a client pays off his debt the longer he will be burdened by debt.

In the world of crypto currency investment you can use this compounding effect, too. For this you need to use special software designed to generate a compounding effect that runs on a 24x7 time frame. This software can be installed on Windows and MacOS computers. It makes use of deposits that are left more than 30 days.

The interest rate is generated by a special kind of mining that could be compared with depositing savings on a savings account for more than a month.

7.2 Track of your crypto currency portfolio

The same way you can track your investments in venture capital opportunities, the same way you should keep a bird's eye on what is happening with your digital assets. You can use complex software, online services or for privacy reasons a locally stored Microsoft Excel sheet. Keep it lean and mean to not loose track of the important aspects of your portfolio.

We use our own portfolio management software for tracking investments in mutual funds and ventures that are not listed on stock markets. Here we see the great value of compact reports that give you the key information and do not gobble up your sight.

This strategy we apply also for our own portfolio of crypto currency investments, as this is a way to know your numbers instead of speculating due to lack of tracking.

7.3 Understand a promising portfolio

When you buy into niche currencies or niche ventures you have to expect certain turbulence. If you believe in the overall vision and benefits the investment will provide to this world, then it is necessary to stick to the purchase as long as possible. My past experience from purchasing shares in the biotechnology and pharmaceutical sector has proven to be forward thinking actions. When discussing these investments 10 years before, my decision was ridiculed as lost money. Ten years later those who did not believe my vision on these investments confirmed my innovative ideas as they sold these stocks with extremely high profits. The key to this success is by evaluating the business model, the vision and the chances that this vision can become a valuable reality.

7.4 Leave a sinking ship with a life vest

Each time we fly the crew tell us how to react in the scenario of a water landing. We read that we should not inflate the life vest inside the cabin.
So how can we apply this to investing in crypto currencies? You need to be able to see if an investment is becoming so unstable that keeping a large portion of your assets in this currency would be insane. You need to know when to move out and when to stay put. Some currencies experience massive storms, which are driven by competing currencies or speculators who want to manipulate the market.

If you want to reduce your risk exposure, you can go along a split strategy. Hereby you only move out part of the assets inside that currency into other currencies. Take into consideration that in certain turbulent times, a currency might be excluded from trading or listings on exchanges.

7.5 Diversify and mitigate risks

Anyone who starts investing in crypto currencies can follow 2 different paths. Some people buy coins and some prefer to invest in the mining of these coins. Of course you can do both. Once you are familiar with the world of crypto currency investing, you can start diversifying your portfolio. This is where purchasing mining services that work on generating different types of crypto currencies can make it easier to build a diverse portfolio. You can start with mainstream coins such as Bitcoin or you can go into niche coins that have an innovative character. It is definitely a good approach to hold Bitcoins and other coins in your portfolio.

I personally spread my risks across Bitcoin, **Dash**, Zcash, **Monero**, **iCambacoin**, Fantomcoin, AEON, **Bitcoin Gold**, Bytecoin, Etherium and other coins. Only in very special situations you should drop out of all currencies and jump into one particular opportunity. If you do not know why you are taking this seldom risk, then you are sure to be loosing your investments at a fast pace.

7.6 Invest in powerful portfolio education

In order to be ahead of the tide, you need to know the trends and how to read subtle signs of opportunities in the world of crypto currencies. You have to read a lot of books and look deep into the associated technologies.

If you do not want to learn from people who are not applying their own strategies then you have to understand the difference between public education and strategic coaching. By using coaching and mastermind education you get insights into the strategies of successful people. These secrets are not often written down in publicly available material. These are trade secrets people have developed over the years based on their mistakes and success stories.

Masterminds are educational events for a small group of 10 to 12 people. These people pay a high price to secure a place at one of these high level sessions where they gain a competitive advantage. This investment into these 2-3 day events will return at a high success rate, if they apply the strategies and knowledge. If they fall to a wrong mind-set then they are only to blame themselves for not taking action when they should have made a strategic decision.

8 Global Taxation Perspectives

Currently different jurisdictions are rating profits from crypto currency exchange gains as either tax free or taxable income. Currently the jurisdictions intending to tax such gains classify them according to following 3 models:

- Income tax
- Company tax
- Capital gains tax

All private individuals and non-incorporated entities are subjected to income tax. This is the case when you receive crypto currencies from mining or being paid in exchange for other transactions (e.g. getting paid for freelance work). Some countries like South Africa see the gains from converting crypto currency into fiat currencies such as USD as income tax related gains.

Company tax applies to corporations (e.g. Limited or incorporated companies), which profit from dealing with crypto currencies. Some jurisdictions place a barrier below which gains are not included in the taxable gains. Capital gains tax will affect people trading crypto currencies for speculative gains. Since some traders place their trading companies in tax havens they try to avoid such taxation. Nevertheless, some jurisdictions differentiate in their level of taxation whether the taxpayer profited from a short-term or long-term investment. Similar situation applies to selling shares in Germany where taxation is fostering a long-term investment strategy.

Following table should offer a brief overview of the current situation. Please keep in mind that jurisdictions constantly look into changing the way they treat crypto currencies from a taxable perspective.

8.1 Taxation in the Americas

Country	Comments	Taxable?
Bolivia	Crypto currencies banned by government due to fear of tax evasion.	Currencies banned!
Brazil	Characterized as "asset" and not a currency. Therefore they apply a capital gains tax of 15%	Capital gains tax

Canada	The 2013 interpretation letter of the Canadian Revenue Agency (CRA) declares crypto currencies as commodities (similar to silver and natural gas).	Business income Or Capital gains
Mexico	The liberal attitude working on a domestic regulatory framework. New measures are being designed.	Awaiting new taxation
USA	IRS considers this as properties (see 8824 form for claims like-kind property exchange). Therefore IRS treats it according to a short-term taxation of capital gains with 25%. Long-term gains lead to a taxation of 0% / 15% / 20% depending on the tax bracket. The Crypto Currency Fairness in Taxation Act (CFTA) would exempt gains below $600 from taxation.	Capital gains taxation

8.2 Taxation in Europe

Country	Comments	Taxation
Austria	Crypto currencies are seen as intangible assets	Income tax
Belgium	Speculation tax was abolished in 2017. There exists no Capital gains tax. High amount of	Wealth tax? Automated can result in Trader tax.

	trading may be classified as professional trading, which is highly taxed.	This income has to be declared!
Finland	Seen as capital gains	Capital gains tax Wealthy tax
Germany	No VAT tax applied. Traders have 800 EUR free capital gains. Any profits above are subject to 25% flat rate on speculative gains. If you made gains from simply holding crypto currency and never moving it, the gains will be tax-free.	Capital gains tax Or Tax-free
Italy	Zero taxation on crypto currencies as of 2017/Q3	Tax-free
Island of Jersey	Treated as income tax as it will be classified as trading. Only mining by companies at a commercial scale can allow for exemption from the rule that costs are not deductible from operational costs.	Income tax
Kazakhstan	Not clearly defined but taxable	Income tax
Poland	The government recognized Bitcoin. They intend to tax Bitcoin profit, which eventually **resulted in banks closing** their Bitcoin related **accounts**.	Capital gains tax? Bitcoin Tax?

Russia	Large mining operations are expecting to be taxed by new government regulation!	Unclear situation
Spain	Profits are to be declared and taxed at a lower rate	Capital gains tax
Sweden	Small mining is rated as hobby, unless it exceeds a threshold and then has to be taxed.	Income/Capital gains tax
Switzerland	Classification as foreign currency. Capital gains taxes are not applied.	Tax-free
United Kingdom	VAT tax repealed in 2014. Most crypto currency transactions are exempt from VAT fees. HM treasury is considering these currencies to be assets as they are not legal currencies. Mining as part of a business will pay corporation tax at standard rate of 20%	Individuals: capital gains tax, but 11,300 GBP are tax-free! Married couples profit from 45200 GBP tax-free crypto currency gains.
Ukraine	This is taxable income	Income tax

8.3 Taxation in Asia

Country	Comments	Taxation
Australia	Crypto currencies are classified as "asset" for the capital gains tax (CGT) purpose (ATO, 2017).	No GST applied anymore. Capital gains taxation

	Double tax on crypto currencies by exempting them from GST taxation. Mining in Australia would result in income whereby operational expenses for mining are deductible from the profits.	
China	The government banned crypto exchanges and ICOs in an attempt to stop money laundering.	Income tax Capital gains tax Company tax
India	Depending on short-term (30%) or long-term (20%) holding a taxpayer will be subject to differing tax rates (Akancha2697, 2017). See for further reference Sec 2(24) of the I-T act! For businesses the Sec 44AD of the I-T Act is of importance.	Capital gains tax Or Business tax
Japan	Crypto currencies as seen as "commodities". The Consumption tax of 8% was removed.	Income tax Capital gains tax Company tax
Singapore	IRAS sees the opportunities of gains via crypto currencies as capital gains.	Capital gains tax
South Korea	Crypto currencies were re-allowed in 2014 with a number of restrictions	Capital gains tax will apply soon

8.4 Taxation in the Middle East

Country	Comments	Taxation
Kuwait	Crypto currencies are not forbidden. Taxation is not fully regulated	Unclear
Israel	Classified crypto currencies as "asset" and therefore they become subject to capital gains.	Capital gains tax
Turkey	Crypto currencies are taxed as financial instruments.	Income tax

8.5 Taxation in Africa

Country	Comments	Taxation
South Africa	The current situation tends towards seeing it as a taxable income	Income tax

9 About the Author

The author of this book has been investing in different kinds of financial opportunities for over 27 years and experienced how wealth grows or declines. Furthermore he developed for over 5 years a special investment management tool for venture capital investors, which have portfolios with over 3 million EUR spread across different industry sectors and nations. Hence, he knows the world of investment from the side of the speculator, the investor and management.

As an innovative entrepreneur he owns a **crypto currency mining service** (www.mineyourwealth.com) for niche currencies. His experience in using all sorts of hardware and software for gradually generating a digital wealth portfolio is being complemented with trading experience. This key knowledge is shared with top clients at mastermind events around the world.

With the help of other industry experts he is taking this technology into other sectors of business. This includes a new solution for applying Blockchain technology in the world of **property investors**. This will open opportunities to <u>buy, flip and levy real estate</u> properties with greater scalability in a global perspective. Several top international property investors are on the board of this niche project.

Christian Bartsch is a speaker and digital forensics expert in niche areas. He often gives presentations of criminal investigations and intelligence strategies for police on behalf of the security authorities. Therefore he is a certified Fraud Examiner (CFE), a German certified forensics expert (DEKRA) and holds several IT related certifications (MCSE, MCSE+I, MCT). Besides providing advice and technical assistance for SME and global players, he also is a special advisor to police and military. Having a security clearance is the necessary by-product of helping authorities to keep our world as safe as possible.

As a serial entrepreneur he has several businesses running in niche sectors. This includes deep mining security with telemetric technology but also in the field of crypto currency mining. These businesses offer technology connections as Blockchain technology is now also entering the mining industry in countries such as Canada. As a forensics expert he is aware that many so called secure block chain technologies are penetrable and therefore do not provide the necessary confidentiality needed for global business or security services.

This is why educating people about investing in crypto currencies also makes it necessary to let people understand how they can use crypto currencies in a safe way. In his recent interview of Apple Co-founder **Steve Wozniak** it was great to get confirmation for an <u>authority in the field of technology</u> innovation that educating all sections of society will help the world benefit from the positive side of innovative forward thinking technologies. It was Steve Wozniak who related his experience in building an understanding for technology in his community to today's anxiety of people <u>because they lack the understanding of crypto currencies</u>.

This compact book on crypto currencies should provide a quick insight whilst avoiding information overflow that will only confuse the reader.

10 Bibliography

Akancha2697, (2017) "Tax on gains from selling Cryptocurrency in India", published 30.11.2017, accessed at **https://blog.ipleaders.in/cryptocurrency-tax/**

ATO (2017), "Treatment of crypto-currencies in Australia – specifically Bitcoin", published 15.12.2017, accessed at https://www.ato.gov.au/General/Gen/Tax-treatment-of-crypto-currencies-in-Australia---specifically-bitcoin/

BadBitcoin (2017), "The Bad List", accessed at: www.badbitcoin.org/thebadlist/index.htm

CoinScamlist (2017), "Coin Scam List", published by CoinScamlist, accessed at: www.coinscamlist.com

CryptoCurrencyFacts (2017), "How do taxes work with Cryptocurrency? Paying taxes on Cryptocurrency in the United States", published by CryptoCurrencyFacts, accessed at http://cryptocurrencyfacts.com/the-basics-of-cryptocurrencies-and-taxes/

Gov.JE (2017) "Cryptocurrency tax treatment", published by the treasury and taxes office, accessed at www.gov.je/taxesmoney/incometax/technical/guidelines/pages/cryptocurrenciestreatment.aspx

Paester, W.M. (2017) (Bitcoin, CryptoCurrency and Taxes: What you need to know", published 29.11.2017, accessed at https://blockonomi.com/cryptocurrency-taxes/

Suberg W. (2016), "One Coin, Much Scam: OneCoin Exposed as Global MLM Ponzy Scheme", Coin Telegraph, published 27.05.2015, accessed at: https://cointelegraph.com/news/one-coin-much-scam-onecoin-exposed-as-global-mlm-ponzi-scheme

Wikipedia (2017), "OneCoin", last edited 30.10.2017, accessed at https://en.wikipedia.org/wiki/OneCoin

CPSIA information can be obtained
at www.ICGtesting.com
Printed in the USA
LVHW021010240521
688318LV00010B/868